Good Grief

G. B. Brock

BookLeaf
Publishing

India | USA | UK

Good Grief © 2022 G. B. Brock

All rights reserved.

No part of this publication may be reproduced, stored in a retrieval system, or transmitted, in any form or by any means, electronic, mechanical, photocopying, recording or otherwise, without the prior written permission of the presenters.

G. B. Brock asserts the moral right to be identified as author of this work.

Presentation by *BookLeaf Publishing*

Web: www.bookleafpub.com

E-mail: info@bookleafpub.com

ISBN: 9789357448734

First edition 2022

ACKNOWLEDGEMENT

I draw inspiration from my past,
so thank you to my roots.

Thank you to my friends.
You hold me in the Loop.

Thank you to the ones who left,
and those of you who stay.

Thank you to my therapist(s).
There've been several along the way.

Thank you to all who teach,
and to all who seek to know.

Thank you to those who're stuck,
and those who always grow.

Thank you to the Great I Am,
whoever you (all?) may be.

Lest I forget, or deny in some future,
sincerest thanks to me.

Love,
G. B.

Back Home

Scrumptious appetizers,
First-class, musical theater.
Wouldn't it be wonderful to show the ones back
home?

Or, maybe they wouldn't care.
Or, worse - they'd think you're arrogant.
Might as well leave it alone.

Business trips, conventions,
Taking the red-eye.
Haven't seen your child in months.

He probably doesn't need you, though.
He'd say so if he did.
You tell him every holiday, "You know I love
you, kid."

On second thought,
You noticed he's getting broad in the back.
Perhaps it's a signal that something's off track?

Rather than accept there's a dysfunction tumor,
You turn a blind eye again,
And cover with humor.

Meanwhile, your youngest stares at a mirror,
Looking for motivation,
And judgment, clearer.

Who am I? Where have I gone?
While you're succeeding,
These are the questions back home.

Boy

One boy in a crowd of women,
A treasured alien,
Sent to help understand the development of
godliness,
In the men surrounding them all.

There was no development particular to the boy.
The boy grew up in the same environment as the
girls his age,
But he was treated differently by the same
environment.

As if boys and girls, or women and men, are two
different things entirely,
Instead of the same with different inborn
capabilities,
Changeable by environment,
In an immediate and cumulative,
Generational way, like many other capabilities.

The beautiful, talented, fatherless-feeling boy
was absorbed,
By others for too long, until he became absorbed
by himself.
He built himself up, smart as a whip.

To cope, to survive, to drift,
Without a clear path.

Insanity

You drove; I was a passenger.
You said we were headed somewhere - the
future, forward.
Why did I stay, rather than take the wheel, jump
out, or demand you stop?

The circles you drove were so grand, so
elaborate.
I thought they were beautiful windings, like
scenic country roads on the path to our
partnership.
I thought vehicle chatter and radio roulette were
the soundtrack of our love.

It took some time for me to learn I was a
hostage.
By the time I realized, you knew enough about
me to convince me otherwise.

The dizzying circles blurred as our speed
increased.
I saw the same abandoned building, our home,
many times before I accepted my fate.

Then, I opened the door, braced for impact, and leapt out.

Enlightened

You float among the stars.
Legs crossed, eyes closed, calm demeanor.
Emotion cannot move you.
You think this is a gift.

A girl waves from Earth.
"Hello, brother! Come down."

You mimic her smile, without opening your
eyes, and speak.
"Soon, sister. After I've finished knowing."

"But, you can never know everything. Please,
come down. I miss you."
Your smile fades, your arms lift, and you chant
unintelligibly.

A transparent barrier grows around you.
Your sister is reminded of a tree ornament and
wishes to extract you.

If she could see you, she thinks, she could
reason with you.
But, the stupid girl is wrong; You are
enlightened.

Half-life

So skinny, your eyes look rounder.
Larger, brighter, urgent.
Even harsh words fall like honey from your lips.

Your mask is alluring,
But nothing to your beautifully penetrable
center.
So, give in already. Give it up.

You fight a losing battle,
Convinced you have the higher ground.
Many try to help you as enemies surround.

Shadows and reflections approach.
Terror colors your veil.
You begin to cower, afraid to fail.

Delusion clouds your perception.
Then medics draw near.
Street shrinks theorize it's only yourself that you
fear.

You never shared the trauma,
That led you to your hill.

The one you refuse to leave, the one you stand
on still.

Others once stood with you,
Basking in your blaze,
Until your demons marched toward them, now a
disordered memory haze.

You threw family and friends toward them,
Thinking they were from Hell.
Do you see now that they were drinking from
your well?

You can still come down, you know?
Everyone waits in the village.
Your homecoming would be a blessing, a cause
for libation spillage.

You will be missed when you're gone,
But must they miss you while you're here?

Recognize the shadows and reflections as your
own,
Comfort them, and come home.

Again

Broken, but all the parts are scattered around us.
Tempted to shout orders, or to pull the wool over
my eyes.

Last time we said we wouldn't do it again.
Wouldn't spin the globe, point our fingers, and
jump in.

Last time you said you couldn't go back and
forth like this.
I couldn't keep aiming for your heart and miss.

It's my time to speak, so listen up my dear.
You're so weak; my love is stronger than your
fear.

We can both be happy; I know that's true.
As for me, I live with or without you.

Crying as I may, dying as I may,
But that'd be true with or without you.

Sleep Paralysis

Awakened by dark silence,
Are eyes even open?
A hazy figure, slowly approaching,
Heavy upon my chest.

No voice, time stopped, limbs numbed.
Victim in dream,
Survivor in life.
Faking reality to keep a frightening world
together.
Fearful that disruption would unleash dreams
into the only known reality.

Must not be victim here in life,
Nor the violent other, an even greater fear.
Perhaps there are other roles,
Ones not seen nor heard along the way.

Ones who could not speak up.
Ones who could not protect
Ones who had limitations.
Ones who now hope for the survivor.

Take my hand, awaken, and you will be suited in
armor.

Stand with the imperfect others.
They hurt how you hurt.
Take their hands, tell them the truth.

We'll defend ourselves together when rarely
needed,
Knowing it's often safe to rest in the company of
friends.

Emaciated

Come back to life!
Limpless, indulgent fool.
Where there is a hole in your heart,
There is one in my mind.

I hurt more, but I knew more, before I imitated
you.
Hopelessly in search of the answer.
What would it take for her to love me,
Something like I thought she loved you?

It would take quite a lot.
I couldn't attain it myself.
I'm not sure any of us could or did.

One last shot.
Speak the truth.
From truth grows love.
We are only in control of so much,
But it's significant.

Medusa

At night, anger has nowhere to go.
It stews, worries, obsesses.
It cannot sleep. It cannot cry.
Not 'till daytime shall there be rest.

Medusa roams the rooms at night.
Her hair hissing, twisting,
And her stare turning soldiers cold as ice.
Best not look directly in her eye.

If she sees your pupil, attack is imminent.
She'll assume her truth has been revealed,
And then the punishment comes.

Swift and painful.
The most intensity felt in weeks.
Desperate, reluctant, hesitant, scared, accepting.

She's magic, casting the most deadly of spells.
Real-life poison ivy, but hardy like kudzu trails.

What is it she wants?
What is it she needs?
Dare to ask, though you may freeze?

Genesis

White trash, unaware.
Balloon my body.
Pull out my hair.

Wrong and ugly.
Pathetic and sad.
Writhe in agony, beg the Lad.

Can you not get up?
Are you so fragile?
Weak and bound, formerly agile.

A titan falls.
Their only pleasure?
Delight in demise; cut and measure.

Scraps of flesh,
Thrown to the fire.
The Void rejoices; they praise their Sire.

Continue the sacrifice.
Beg for His voice.
When you've killed all you love, deny it was
choice.

Little Light

She knows you're talented.
She wants you to keep it under wraps,

Shine, little light.
Overwhelm her senses.
She's so dull, got up all her defenses.
(You know, she's defenseless.)

You shine, I shine, we shine.

She knows you're a tough one.
She wants you to serve her agenda.

Blind, little light.
Pierce her failing vision.
Defend yourself,
From her impending fission.

You shine, I shine, we shine.

Sea

Gnarled waves crash, seething.
Breaking, their roars fade into the silent clouds.
Anger remains.

A chorus of muted agony,
stronger than any army,
cries out helplessly among the sprinkled, smiling
beachgoers.

Mighty, but confined.
Admired, but used.
Alive, but objectified.

Believe

I saw the most beautiful girl in the world.
She said we could go upstairs for a while.

But I believe in something bigger than me,
and I believe in something bigger than her.

She looked up to my eyes and offered her heart,
But I could not imagine any future worth it to
me.

I fell in love a million years ago.
I fell in love with you.
I believe in something bigger than all of us, and
it's love.

Bloodletting

Running in tear-like streams,
Down legs draped by a white,
Linen nightgown topped with ruffles.

Losing strength,
Face whitening,
Requiring nourishment.

What did you need?
What could I give?
I can tell you it hurt.

Transfusion.
Fixed.
Parasite.
Detach.
Please, detach.

Void

Falling or flying?
For moments, I can't tell.
I feel sick in the best way,
Swept off my feet,
A little bit scared.

Haunting how captivating that can be,
How much we fear ourselves,
When we're told we're wrong,
Just for being.

A hot flame you're afraid to touch,
So you just stare,
Run away,
Or extinguish it.

Tempted to give in and love yourself,
To just let yourself be,
But having not known love yourself,
How do you start?

As wrong as I've been, or so I've been told,
Internalized, my thoughts turn to doubt.
Would I go off the rails?
Would my actions hurt someone?

Would I lose myself?

It's difficult to forgive and trust again.
To trust that I know better now,
That I can better protect myself now,
That I can be kinder to myself now.
Awareness, balance, consistency.

Ivan the Terrible

Maniacal laughter.
Out of a funk.
Lies over-ripened, molded, and stunk.

The upside-down room,
Where pancakes delight.
Confirmation of something not right.

Faced with mortality.
Collapsed on yourself.
Cleaned your bookcase, put us back on the shelf.

Play with your dolls.
Make them war 'til they crack.
Don't feign surprise when they can't love you
back.

You've robbed them of wealth,
Dignity, and respect.
You'll never love them, they learn to expect.

You killed your son, his son, all in your path.
You'll die without lineage, claiming brilliance in
math.

What is it that lonely does?
You stare at dark portals, waiting for buzz.

The further you sink,
The longer it takes.
Until, for a moment, your interest awakes.

Is there something for you there?
Something to win?
Money, glory, some other sin?

Like it or not,
Your dolls are real.
And, under your rule, we cannot heal.

To spite your leg,
You cut off your thigh.
We'll no longer beg for scraps; goodbye.

Meet Me Halfway?

Seeing the two of them together, betrayal.
But they aren't so different, are they?

Seeing the four of us ripped apart,
Not down any convenient seam,
But across reality and reflections,
Stone and shadows.

What is illusion, and does it matter?

How much of the madness will be re-written as
harmless theatrics,
A funhouse of the most beguiling?

The kind that dazzles you with sparkles and
dizzying dances,
But leaves you pleading for escape once
ensnared?

Shot

Thank you for the time you gave me,
To figure things out.

Thank you for keeping the violence only in your
dreams,
For allowing me to survive.

I know you were a trained assassin,
And I respect your restraint.
You did better than you might've,
Not because of your potential,
But because of your training.

I felt you follow me,
I feared you knew my thoughts.
I had to hide them, too,
For so long and from so many,
That I hardly knew them myself.

You are not the same as your predecessors,
I see that now.
Can we start new?
Me trusting you?
A little at a time?

Sapling

The unloved pluck intently,
strand by strand,
until their commander is threadbare.

A decomposing core exposed,
gazers speculate post-mortem.

A seedling emerges from the metastasized mass,
unseen, unknown, struggling to grow among the
rot.

For moons, too small to see more than ruin or
sky.
Look up, wonder why,
or look around - haunted ground.

Time sends gentle rain to cleanse the seeking
sapling.
A symphony of delicate drops emerges from a
long-forgotten forest.

Look around now, find comfort.
Look down now, find roots.
Look up now, find hope.

Exodus

Can you hear me, my people?
Do your hearts still stir?
Your silence has deafened me.

Why must I call out for your help?
Was I not the one you worshipped?
Every eye I search is hollow.

The weakest voice whispers,
"Here, I'm here."
A beaten mass struggles to lift their head.

"Thank you for coming."
Tears flood their cheeks.
"Hope kept me alive, though I spent my faith
foolishly."

You were robbed, my child.
Where are your caretakers?
Come with me; your journey begins now.

Rose Glass

Up in the cabinet,
All the way at the top.
No one could reach you,
Except the few misfits placed alongside you.

Brown and orange Tupperware, a stained old
colander, and an empty tea jug.

You loved all the junk because they were your
friends,
Not junk at all,
Just those on the mend.

On the mend from a stain, a fall, or a bruise,
Too wide for the shelf,
Too unappealing to display.

Some of her favorites, you all were,
The one who jumped up on the counter,
And climbed to the top.

www.ingramcontent.com/pod-product-compliance
Lightning Source LLC
LaVergne TN
LVHW021340200726
843509LV00014B/2604